Sophie's Superpower

Written by Dawn Crowle and Rhiannon Jones

Illustrated by Rhiannon Jones

Sophie had been struggling with reading and writing at school.

She didn't understand why she found it so much harder than the other children in her class.

Sophie's parents and teacher realised she was struggling with her learning.

After going to see a specialist and doing tests with Sophie they found out she had dyslexia.

WAS?

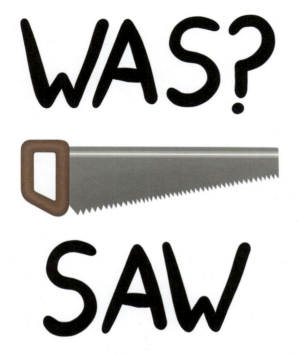

SAW

WICH
SHOWT
LOOKT

Sometimes words looked different to her.

She spelled words as they sounded.

3

Wetookthedogtothepark
forarunaround.Ithrew
hisballandhebroughtit
back,hehadalotoffun.

The dog ran away

Words would blend together and leave no gaps.

Letters would move around the page as she tried to read.

Although Sophie was happy to know why she struggled at school, she couldn't help but feel different from her friends. Every night before bed Sophie would read a book to her Mum, but she felt frustrated that she sometimes got stuck on a word.

'I don't want to be dyslexic anymore Mummy. I want to be NORMAL!'
'Sophie, dyslexia is your superpower! You might struggle with reading and writing but you are amazing in lots of other ways!.'

The next day Sophie and her sister Ruby were playing with clay. Sophie was having a lot of fun, but she noticed Ruby was struggling. 'Would you like me to help you?'
Sophie asked. 'Yes please! I want to make a rabbit to take to school but it's too hard.' Ruby said.

Sophie helped Ruby to make some tall ears and a big fluffy tail for her clay rabbit.

'You're my hero!' Ruby beamed at her rabbit before hugging her sister tight.

That night before bed Sophie read another book to her Mum. There were some words she couldn't understand as she read and she found herself feeling frustrated again.

'Remember, dyslexia is a superpower!' Her Mum said.

'Do you have a superpower Mummy?' She asked.

'Yes, I also have dyslexia.' Her Mum told her.

'But you can read and write well.' Said Sophie.

'I still struggle sometimes but I practised a lot and each time I got better at it. That's why you need to keep practising as much as you can, that's how you'll improve.'

Sophie practised reading and writing at school and at home.

She started to notice that she could read some of the sentences she found difficult, and spell some of the longer words she used to find hard.

16

Her teacher noticed the improvement and gave her a special award for her hard work.

The teacher announced that Friday would be dress up day at school and every pupil needed to decide what they wanted to dress up as.

'Have you decided what you're going to dress up as on Friday?' Sophie's Mum asked her.

'Yes.' Sophie replied with a smile.

Sophie spent the week gathering materials and making her costume.

On Friday morning Sophie got dressed into her costume and ran downstairs to show her family.

'What have you decided to go as?' Ruby asked her.
'Myself.' Sophie said proudly.

At school Sophie was proud to tell everyone all about her costume, and all about her real life superpower, dyslexia.